3058
PAC
Tel

VISUAL SOURCE
EQUALITY

H+H

Abstract

3 Week

Order details PO0224478/TI
RL 18·11·05 CR   12.99.

UNDERSTANDING IMMIGRATION

A Multicultural World

Iris Teichmann

FRANKLIN WATTS
LONDON•SYDNEY

First published in 2005 by Franklin Watts
96 Leonard Street, London EC2A 4XD

Franklin Watts Australia
Level 17/207 Kent Street
Sydney NSW 2000

Series editor: Rachel Cooke
Series Design: Simon Borrough
Picture research: Diana Morris

Dewey Classification: 305.8
A CIP catalogue record for this book is
available from the British Library.

ISBN: 0 7496 6108 9

Printed in Malaysia

Acknowledgements
Alexander the Great's story, p.10, Michael Bakaoukas,
"Tribalism and Racism among the Ancient Greeks",
Anistoriton, Vol. 9, March 2005; China's story, p.11,
Herbert A Giles, "The Civilization of China",
Historical Text Archive 2003, historicaltextarchive.
com; The Wichí Indians' story, p.12, Survival
International, www.survival-international.org; The
Norwegian Americans' story, p.13, The Norwegian-
American Historical Association, Northfield, MN,
USA; Abigail Adams' story, p.14, Laurie Carter Noble,
Abigail Adams, Unitarian Universalist Historical
Society; Thomas Macaulay's story, p.15, "Minute on
Indian Education", humanitas.ucsb.edu; Liang
Qichao's story, p.17, "Selected Memoirs of Travels in
the New World", xroads.virginia.edu; A Greek
Australian's story, p.18, Alexandra Holvea, "Current
Trends of the Linguistic and Cultural Values of the
Greek Australian Community in South Australia",
International Education Journal, Vol. 4, No. 4, 2004;
Vince Reid's story, p.19, www.bbc.co.uk/history;
Malika's story, p.21, "The Integration Paper: The
Contributors", For Diversity Against Discrimination,
Journalist Award 2004 campaign, www.ja04.stop-
discrimination.info; Zerife's story, p.22,
www.denmark.dk; Moris Farhi's story, p.23, *Exiled
Ink!*, No. 1, 2003; Hansa's story, p.24, *Hansa's Indian
Vegetarian Cookbook*, Hansa's Publications, 2000;
Tsoarnelo's story, p.25, www.rage.co.za; A typical
story, p.26, www.bangla.ca; Aïcha's story, p.27, Aïcha
Benaïssa, *Née en France*, 2000, Pocket; John A Powell's
story, p.28, California News Reel, 2003,
www.pbs.org/race; Sylvia's story, p.29, The Legal Aid
Society Employment Law Center; Dyab Abou Jahjah's
story, p.32, "The Many Faces of Islam", *Time*,
08/01/05; Joanne's story, p.33, Joanne Richmond, *My
Heritage is Franco-American*, Unitarian University
History Society, www.uua.org; Pavi's story, p.34,
www.excelsis.cc/weblog/pavi/archives/cat_people.php;
Fadime's story, p.35, www.cnn.com, 5/2/2002, and
Aftonbladet, 04/02/2002; Vaira Vike-Freiberga's story,
p.36, United Nations High Commissioner for
Refugees; Jennifer's story, p.37, Jun-yung Ahn, *Korea
Daily News*, 12/05/03; Jette's story, p.38, Jette Englund
Smith, 1997, unbound.intrasun.tcnj.edu/archives/
government/old/american.html; Shane's story, p.39,
Aetna Smith, "Identity Squeeze: What Irks Mixed-
Race Americans in Daily Life", www.jru.columbia.edu;
Camilla's story, p.40, Camilla Pedersen, "The Search
for Normal", www.onvik.com.

Photographic credits: Vicky Alhadett/Lebrecht/
Alamy: p.23. Archivberlin Fotoagentur GmbH/Alamy:
p.33. Craig Aurness/Corbis: p.18. David Brauchli/
Sygma/Corbis: p.21. David Butow/Saba/Corbis: p.37.
Peter Casolino/Alamy: p.25. Jackie Chapman/
Photofusion: p.27. Coo-ee Picture Library: p.16.
Christopher Cormack/Impact Photos: p.32. Michael
Fresco/Rex Features: p.35. Sally Greenhill/Sally &
Richard Greenhill: p.41. Richard Greenhill/Sally &
Richard Greenhill: pp.9, 20, 24. Ute Klaphake/
Photofusion: front cover b, pp.2, 3, 4, 45, 46, 47. Erich
Lessing/Louvre, Paris/AKG Images: p.10bl. Gunter
Marx Photography/Corbis: p.22. Ulli Michel/Corbis:
p.28. Maggie Murray/Photofusion: p.26. Naglestock.
com/Alamy: p.11. Joanne O'Brien/Photofusion: pp.29,
31. John Palmer/Survival International: p.12.
Pinacoteca Capitolina, Palazzo Conservatori, Rome,
Italy/Giraudon/Bridgeman Art Library: p.10tr.
Popperfoto: p.19. Ulrike Preuss/Photofusion: front
cover t, pp.8, 34. J.B. Russell/Panos Pictures: p.40.
Rykoff Collection/ Corbis: p.17. Christa Stadtler/
Photofusion/Alamy: p.36. David Turnley/Corbis: p.39.
Eileen Tweedy/Terry Engell Gallery/Art Archive: p.13.
Upperhall/Robert Harding: p.15. Deng Yai: p.30. Yale
Center for British Art, Paul Mellon Collection,
USA/Bridgeman Art Library: p.14. Michael S.
Yamashita/Corbis: p.38.

Contents

What is multiculturalism?   8

Cultural encounters in the past   10

Into the melting pot   16

Our multicultural world   20

The fight for equality   28

Understanding difference   32

A question of identity   36

The multicultural future   40

Glossary   42

Web connections   43

Index   44

What is multiculturalism?

A crowd enjoys an open-air concert. Our societies are made up of an increasingly diverse mix of people.

What is culture?

Most of us use the word "culture" to describe activities in the worlds of music, art, literature and film. But culture is much more than that. It is the way of life that is passed on from one generation to another. It includes the language we learn when we grow up and the customs, ideas, values and types of behaviour that our families teach us about. Our culture changes as we learn about other people's ideas and values.

Becoming multicultural

Today, many of us live alongside people from very different cultures – our societies have become multicultural ones. A multicultural society is one in which people from different cultures live together. Cultural diversity tends to be promoted and celebrated in these societies, but there are still considerable differences in the way people from different racial and cultural backgrounds are treated, especially if they are in a minority.

Old news

The modern multicultural world has developed as a result of immigration patterns in the 19th and 20th centuries. Starting in the 1800s, an unprecedented number of people moved from eastern and central Europe – and later from all over the world – to seek a better life, freedom and security in the West (North America, Australasia and western Europe). But there is nothing new about multiculturalism itself. Throughout history, civilisations have influenced other civilisations through conquest, migration and trade.

Culture clash

History shows that where people with different physical appearances, behaviour and beliefs live together there is almost always tension. At a basic human level, this arises because people are fearful or suspicious of those from other cultures and races, and can find it difficult to tolerate them or consider them their equal. Tensions, however, can hide the positive aspects of different people living together. From the way we eat and shop to our beliefs and art, multicultural societies enrich our lives.

Many Western cities are multicultural places, where people from different cultures tolerate and learn from each other.

AS A MATTER OF FACT

Race: A group of people with common physical characteristics. The Caucasian race, for example, refers to people of white skin colour of European, Middle Eastern and North African descent.

Ethnic group: Each race has many different ethnic groups. In turn, each ethnic group has its own culture, ancestry and homeland, and often language, too.

Ethnic minority: An ethnic group that forms only one part of a larger group in society.

For example, black people form an ethnic minority in the USA and the UK, while white people are an ethnic minority in South Africa and the Middle East.

Nation: A community of people – who may belong to different ethnic groups – that shares a common territory and often, although not always, has its own government. It may also share a common culture. For example, people of many different backgrounds celebrate Thanksgiving Day in the USA.

9

Cultural encounters in the past

Cultural exchange

Different cultures have been influencing one another for thousands of years. The ancient Greeks colonised Italy and parts of Asia Minor (modern-day Turkey), spreading their culture while at the same time encouraging trade. From their home in Italy, the Romans set up colonies as far away as Britain. The Romans encouraged their subjects to adopt Roman culture. If people did not give up their own customs and beliefs they remained foreigners in society, but they were still tolerated.

Barbarians and Greeks

Like the Romans, the ancient Greeks had a notion of difference based more on culture than physical appearance. They viewed anyone who did not speak their language as "barbarian". But if foreigners did learn the language and adopted Greek customs, they were not only able to integrate better but also able to gain status in the same way as any other Greek.

This Greek vase, from about 480 BCE, depicts two market traders. Trade is an ancient way for cultures to come into contact with each other.

ALEXANDER THE GREAT'S STORY: EARLY MULTICULTURALISM

Alexander the Great (356–323 BCE) expanded the empire of the ancient Greeks and spread Greek civilisation and culture. In 326 BCE he reached India, where he made this appeal:

"I do not separate people as many narrow-minded others do into Greeks and Barbarians. I'm not interested in the origin of race of citizens. I only distinguish them on the basis of their virtue. For me each good foreigner is a Greek and each bad Greek is a barbarian... For my part I consider all, whether they be white or black, equal, and I would like you to be not only the subjects of my commonwealth, but also participants and partners."

10

Absorbing other cultures

Between 206BCE and 220CE, China's emperors, from the largest ethnic group, the Han, also unified different groups of people into one dominant culture. As a result, people from outside the Chinese empire were viewed with suspicion and even considered a threat to its culture. Both during the Han dynasty and many times after, China was influenced by influxes of people from outside its borders, but this fearful attitude towards outsiders continued up to the modern age.

CHINA'S STORY: GETTING USED TO THE "FOREIGN DEVILS"

Writing in the early 20th century, the English scholar of Chinese language and culture Herbert A Giles described the Chinese attitude to foreigners:

"The Chinaman may love you, but you are a devil all the same. It is most natural that he should think so. For generation upon generation China was almost completely isolated from the rest of the world. The people of her vast empire grew up under influences unchanged by contact with other peoples. Their ideals became stereotyped from want of other ideals to compare with, and possibly modify, their own... Then the foreign devil [Europeans] burst upon the scene... Small wonder that little children are terrified at these strange beings, and rush shrieking into their cottages as the foreigner passes by."

The Great Wall of China runs for about 6,700 kilometres across northern China. It was completed in the 3rd century BCE to protect the country from invaders.

11

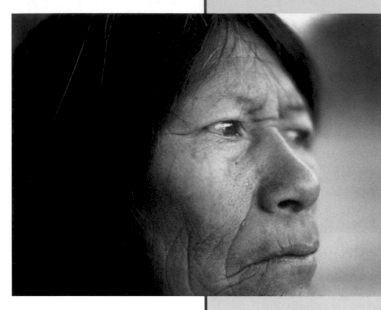

A modern-day Wichí Indian.

THE WICHÍ INDIANS' STORY: LOSING LAND AND LIVELIHOOD

In the 17th century European colonialists invaded the land of the Wichí Indians in Argentina. A modern-day Wichí tells what happened to his ancestors:

"We call the colonists *ahatai*, which is like our words for 'spirit of the dead' (*ahat*) and for 'the devil' (*ahataj*). The ahatai ... used deceit and violence in order to take [our land] from us. At first they deceived our leaders by telling them that they wanted to borrow some grasslands for just a few months in order to graze their cattle. Our ancestors were not mean about land and the leaders allowed the new arrivals to use it for a short while in exchange for some tobacco and beef and metal tools. But, by the end of a year, the ahatai had built houses and corrals; they had moved all their livestock onto the land, including horses, goats, sheep and pigs, and they had no intention of leaving."

New World conquerors

From the 16th century onwards, European powers built empires by conquering territory overseas and exploiting the land and resources of indigenous peoples. The Europeans' initial contact with native tribes was often violent, but both sides tried to benefit from each other. The colonialists needed to communicate with tribal leaders to acquire food and learn about the land and its resources. The tribal leaders, in turn, were often keen to obtain goods from the Europeans, which could raise their status and power.

Exploitation

For the most part, the colonising Europeans viewed the natives they encountered as people without culture or true religion, referring to them as "savages". The colonialists saw themselves as a superior culture, and their missionaries tried to convert the natives to Christianity. As different European powers competed for their slice of colonies overseas, indigenous peoples increasingly suffered. Their land was taken away, they were often forced to work in appalling conditions, and their access to food and other resources could be severely restricted.

12

To settle or not

The European colonialists were for the most part interested in exploiting resources and less interested in setting up permanent settlements. In contrast, North America was regarded as a virtual wilderness that was ideal for settlement and development. The first Europeans to arrive there were the British, but other settlers soon followed. The majority were motivated to start a new life and to shape a new identity. Others, however, found life hard and tried to maintain their own cultural identity.

THE NORWEGIAN AMERICANS' STORY: A DIFFICULT START

In 1847 the Norwegian Consul-General Adam Løvenskjold visited Wisconsin in the USA, where about 7,500 Norwegians lived. Many of the settlers he visited complained about their new life in America. Løvenskjold wrote that the settlers were living **"to a large extent in sod huts almost underground, with only the roofs projecting above the surface"**.

Many had not yet learned English and knew little about American life nor its political institutions. He added that other Americans called the settlers "Norwegian Indians", comparing them to the Native American Indians whom they looked down on.

Future North American settlers prepare for their long journey from Europe in the early 1600s. Many settlers escaped religious persecution in Europe to build new communities overseas.

13

An English lord hunting with his black servant, in a painting from about 1765. Many more black people worked for white masters in the Caribbean and the Americas than Europe.

The slave trade

Colonialisation brought with it the enslavement of African people to work on plantations in the European colonies. When Africans were first shipped to North America, they worked alongside poor European labourers under the same harsh conditions. But towards the end of 17th century, colonial laws began to separate the African slaves from the European labourers.

Distinguishing black from white

Slavery became increasingly important for the European economies, and African slaves began to be referred to as "negroes". In Europe and the Americas a clear distinction arose between whites, who had privileges, rights and power, and blacks, who had none. To justify their denial of equality and rights to black people, white Europeans and Americans developed theories that blacks were inferior to whites. In the late 1700s it was down to individuals like Abigail Adams to speak out for black people.

14

ABIGAIL ADAMS'S STORY: SPEAKING OUT

Abigail Adams (1744–1818) was the wife of the second president of the USA, John Adams. When a black servant boy, the son of a freed slave, came to her asking to learn to write, she enrolled him in a local school. In response to criticisms of her action she wrote:

"[The boy is] a freeman as much as any of the young men and merely because his face is black, is he to be denied instruction? How is he to be qualified to procure a livelihood? I have not thought it any disgrace to my self to take him into my parlor and teach him both to read and write."

THOMAS MACAULAY'S STORY: CULTURAL SUPERIORITY

In 1843 the British government sent the politician and writer Thomas Macaulay to India to decide on the language for a national education system. Some argued that Indian people should be taught in Sanskrit or Arabic, but Macaulay insisted on English, at least for the most able Indians who would work for the British government in India.

"The dialects commonly spoken among the natives of this part of India, contain neither literary nor scientific information, and are, moreover, so poor and rude that, until they are enriched from some other quarter, it will not be easy to translate any valuable work into them... We must at present do our best for a class who may be interpreters between us and the millions whom we govern; a class of persons, Indian in blood and colour, but English in taste, in opinions, in morals, and in intellect."

Modern-day Calcutta, India's largest city. English remains one of the most widely used languages in India – a remnant of the time when Britain ruled the country.

A difficult legacy

Some people argue that the discrimination against black people during the slave trade, when it was the norm for white people to have power and rights over black people, still influences Western attitudes towards race. Others argue that these attitudes predate the slave trade, because they were clearly held by the European conquerors of South America, southern Asia (including India) and Africa. Many European colonialists wrote that native tribes had "lax morals", and that they were uncultured.

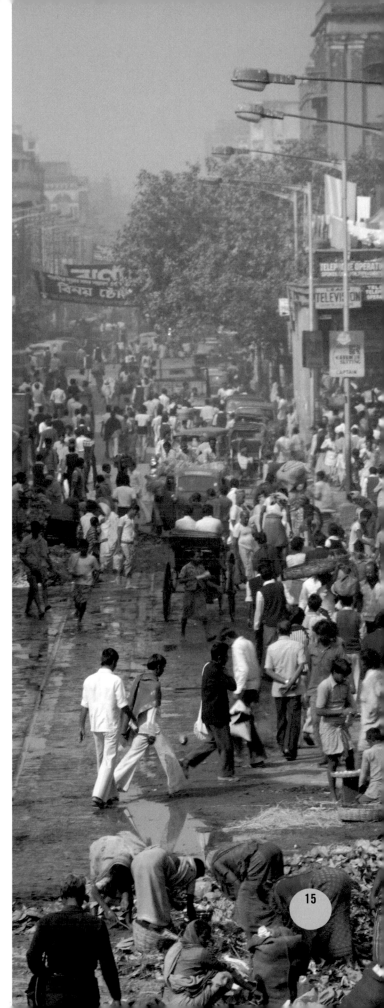

15

Into the melting pot

In the 19th and early 20th centuries millions of people from southern and eastern Europe attempted to put poverty and persecution behind them, moving to the USA, Canada, Australia and South America. The arrival of so many different people alongside the mix of earlier immigrants meant that the USA, in particular, became known as a "melting pot" of different nationalities and cultures.

AS A MATTER OF FACT

The phrase "melting pot" implies that, on arrival in the USA, immigrants left their own customs, traditions, beliefs and values behind to form a new culture shared by everyone else. Historians, however, have shown that this was not the case. Different groups had different experiences of adapting to American life. Many immigrants settled alongside people from their home countries, and kept their own culture as much as possible. The era of mass immigration led to the building up of ethnic communities in the USA that still largely exist today.

Southern European immigrants arriving at Port Melbourne, Australia, in 1948.

Making it for themselves

The 19th- and early 20th-century European immigrants were different from the earlier northern European settlers. Many did not intend to stay in their new countries, but to return home once they had saved up enough money. They often identified with the immigrant dream of making a career for themselves, but were unlikely to search for a new identity in the way earlier European settlers had done. They kept very much to their own culture and community and, as a result, found it harder to be accepted by earlier immigrant groups.

16

Racial prejudice

The Chinese were one of the first non-European peoples to migrate to Australia and North America in search of work. Because they looked different and had a very different culture, Chinese people were not easily accepted into their new societies.

Newspapers reflected this hostility with stories about their "peculiar" habits. Prejudice, as well as the problems many Chinese had learning English, meant that they relied on their own communities for support and comfort as much as possible.

This postcard from about 1900 depicts New York's Chinese district.
Today, "Chinatowns" all over the world are vibrant and bustling places.

SCENE IN CHINATOWN, NEW YORK

LIANG QICHAO'S STORY: THE NEED TO OPEN UP

In the early 20th century the Chinese scholar Liang Qichao (1873–1929) visited communities of his fellow countrymen and women in the USA. He complained in his writings about the way in which they kept to themselves rather than learning more about their American counterparts.

"Chinese can be clansmen but not citizens. I believe this all the more since my travels in America. There you have those who have left villages and taken on the character of individuals and come and go in the most free of the great cities ... and still they cling to the family and clan systems to the exception of other things."

17

A Mexican American family in the 1970s. Immigrant communities and families are often very close knit.

A new generation

The mass movement of people to the USA, Canada and Australia could not continue for ever. By the early 20th century governments began to restrict immigrant numbers. Immigrant communities did not grow to the extent they had done previously, but for new arrivals, they provided an important network of support and opportunities.

Many immigrants stayed within the cultural boundaries of their families and close-knit communities. They worked hard and saved money in order to provide their children with an education, so that they in turn would be able to move up into professional jobs. Immigrant communities were also known for providing the next generation with inspiration and values that emphasised that they could achieve more if they worked hard.

18

A GREEK AUSTRALIAN'S STORY: CHANGING ATTITUDES

Hard work was not the only reason why some immigrants kept themselves to themselves. As this Greek Australian writer shows, prejudice was another major factor:

"In the 70s the racial conflict was terrible with regards being a pupil at school or finding a job. Even when working, it was very difficult with racism. Nowadays life has changed, the country is more multicultural and has accepted the migrants more so than then. As a child and teenager I found it difficult because I knew I was different than the majority, however, there were enough of us around not to feel too isolated. As I grew older, in my mid to late teens, I began to appreciate this difference and felt proud to come from such a culturally diverse background."

The European experience

In the rush to rebuild Europe after the Second World War (1939–45), countries such as France and Britain accepted large numbers of immigrants from their former colonies. Indians, Pakistanis and African Caribbeans were among the peoples who came to the UK in search of work and new lives, while immigrants from Algeria came to France, fleeing economic hardship and civil war.

New arrivals from the Caribbean disembark from the *Empire Windrush* at Tilbury docks in England, in 1948.

VINCE REID'S STORY: ON THE WINDRUSH

Vince Reid was one of the 2,000 Caribbean people that journeyed to Britain on board the ship the *Empire Windrush* in June 1948 – the largest arrival of Caribbeans to the UK at the time.

"My parents brought me on the Windrush – I had no choice in the matter. They didn't have to – it was obvious they came in search of a better life, better opportunities. It was quite a devastating experience. I was thirteen when I arrived so I wasn't a man, I was a boy... I went to school in Kings Cross. I never associated with white people in any significant degree, and then at school I came across real hostility ... to say I had no friends for several years wouldn't be far from the truth."

19

Our multicultural world

The benefits of multiculturalism

Modern Western societies benefit from multiculturalism in lots of ways. Some benefits are economic – many immigrants have a very strong work ethic and may even take on jobs that other people are not willing to do. Some benefits are cultural, in terms of the creative talents and traditions of different peoples, which often intermingle and emerge as new forms. Most important, perhaps, are the social benefits. Living alongside people from different backgrounds helps broaden horizons and breaks down prejudices.

Old problems

Prejudice stills exists, however. Since the early 20th century most Western countries have experienced waves of negative public opinion and hostility towards ethnic minorities, usually at times when immigration is particularly high. Much of this hostility is directed at newly arrived immigrants, with local populations regarding them as a threat to their jobs and the stability of their culture.

Unlike 50, or even 20 years ago, most of us are used to living alongside people from different backgrounds.

Serving the whole community

The existence of different cultural and ethnic groups in societies has meant that governments now think about how to serve their multiethnic communities better. The police and other public services, for example, work to ensure that everyone can benefit from their services. Public information is translated into many languages so that people with little knowledge of the country's main language know how to vote, to access welfare services, report a crime and get medical care.

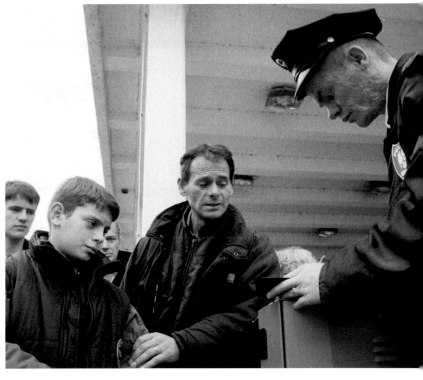

Kosovan refugees at an Albanian border checkpoint. The arrival of refugees and immigrants in the West can lead to hostility and racism.

Gaining trust

By trying to cater for their diverse communities, public services in developed countries have also tried to gain more trust with different ethnic groups by employing people from these communities. This increases understanding on both sides and promotes better participation of ethnic minority groups in public life. Problems persist, however. Police forces in developed countries, for example, are often criticised for unfairly picking on people from ethnic minorities.

MALIKA'S STORY: BECOMING ACCEPTED

Malika was born in Morocco and went to Denmark in 1990. She found her first job despite speaking very little Danish. She now works as a bus driver, and drives wearing a Muslim headscarf. Often, passengers have stared at her, but Malika has learnt to deal with it and has found her new job experience very positive.

"I know that many people are a little surprised to see a Muslim woman with a headscarf behind the wheel. That is why I take pains to make some friendly remarks to the passengers. I want to set a good example."

LRS: Somerset College

21

Learning about the world

From books to music, the arts express what it is like to live in a multicultural society. They also promote cultural diversity. Today, for example, there are many plays, films and novels that document the personal stories of immigrants and refugees, and how they have coped with leaving their countries and building a new life elsewhere. Cities across the developed world offer a vast selection of cultural events either about other cultures or organised and performed by people from ethnic minority communities.

An Indian singer at the Vancouver Folk Festival in Canada.

Learning about oneself

For many people, being artistically creative can help them cope with the transition of their lives and to explore their own cultural identities. This is particularly the case with immigrant communities or people from ethnic minorities. Art can be a way to define how a person feels about him or herself, as well as the means to express hope, anxiety or frustration with their surroundings. For Zerife, taking part in a play was a useful way to build up her confidence.

22

ZERIFE'S STORY: WE ARE!

Zerife and her older sister, alongside other members of Denmark's ethnic minority communities, were invited to take part in a play called *We Are*, at a well-known theatre in the capital city, Copenhagen. The play told the audience about the actors' lives and dreams in Denmark.

"My family is Kurdish, and we come from Turkey. The story I told in the show was my grandmother's story. She has lived in Denmark for many years, but never felt really at home here. The project has definitely changed me as a person, made me more mature and better at working in a group....What we've been doing there has given me a lot of self confidence, and it's cool to be in that world where things are so different."

Mutual influence

But art is not just about the individual artist and the messages it gives out to its audience. Different art forms from different cultures continuously influence each other. A Western musician might like certain sounds or elements of music from Africa and incorporate these into his or her own music. On the other hand, artists from different cultures living in the West will be influenced by what they see, hear and observe in their new surroundings. Artists are often inspired by the very richness and diversity different cultural art forms can bring.

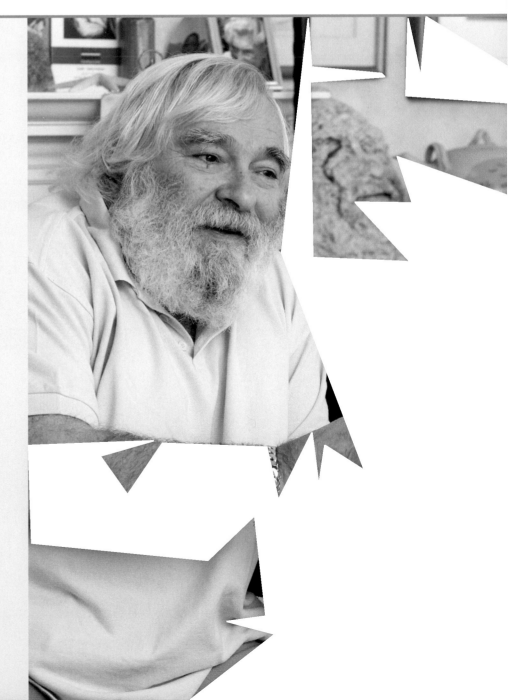

MORIS FARHI'S STORY: THE FORCE OF WRITING

The writer Moris Farhi was born in Turkey in 1935, but has lived and worked in the UK for many years. In an interview he described his feelings about his identity:

"I've been [in Britain] now 48 years and I still look upon myself as a Turk. You are really formed in your early youth. Most of the Turkish traditions still remain with me... I write mainly about persecuted people and persecuted cultures. I believe that pluralism is our greatest wealth, that the more cultures we have, the more languages we speak, the more literatures we produce, the more we can interact with these different cultures, the more humanity will benefit."

World food

Today more than ever we enjoy food and goods from around the world and are able to go out to Chinese, Vietnamese, Mexican, Indian, Middle Eastern and many other different types of restaurants. Ethnic shops and restaurants are vitally important businesses, serving and employing the local community. They also bring part of their culture to a wider audience, and introduce people to new tastes and ideas in cooking.

A food stall at a festival offers a mixed ethnic menu.

HANSA'S STORY: A MIXED CULTURAL CUISINE

Hansa's family – originally from Gujarat in India – worked in Uganda until they had to flee the dictatorship there in 1971. Hansa, her parents and five sisters and brothers ended up in Leeds, England. In 1978 she met her husband who was from a different Indian caste. They married in secret, against both their parents' wishes. When her two sons were born, Hansa started organising Indian cookery demonstrations, food stalls and fundraising events in her community. She eventually opened up a very successful Gujarati vegetarian restaurant in Leeds with the support of her husband.

"[My dishes] draw together my experiences as a Hindu living as a vegetarian in the West. My Indian, East African and English upbringing all influence the recipes and the choice of ingredients, producing dishes that are a little different and reflect my individual tastes. I hope that they provide an experience that is both physically and mentally satisfying."

24

Sporting success

But it is not just in the arts or cuisine that people in multicultural societies benefit from the different groups living there. Sport is one area where different people bring different talents and levels of motivation. In the USA, for example, African Americans have achieved great success in athletics, basketball and boxing, among other sports. Some suggest that black people are better athletes than white people. But experts point out that black athletes train as hard as anyone and often have to overcome social disadvantages to get to the top.

Women basketball players in the USA.

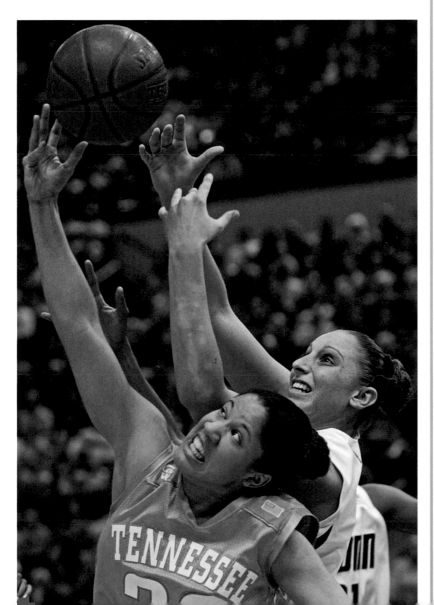

TSOARNELO'S STORY: STRIVING TO BE THE BEST

Tsoarnelo Pholo lives in Johannesburg, South Africa. She is a talented hockey player who has played for the South African junior national team. Since South Africa has emerged from its Apartheid past, Tsoarnelo is among a relatively small number of black athletes to have represented her country.

"As a black woman, with the colour issue we're close. Our vice-captain is a coloured player. She's been with the team for about five years, great young player, barely 22. We only went with one black female athlete out of 104 athletes to the Olympics, which was me. I guess sometimes when people say you were the black [female] athlete, it's an honour but I expect more players of colour."

When asked about South Africa's quota system, which requires that a certain number of black athletes have to be in a national team, Tsoarnelo said:

"My view is that it undermines me as a hockey person. I don't want to play hockey because I'm black and make the team because I'm black. I'd like to think I'm in the team because I'm one of the top five strikers in the country. It drives me to perform, I should be concentrating on my game. I think we should get the quota system at junior level so that the development structures grow."

25

Multicultural schools

Many schools in developed countries, particularly in inner-city areas, educate young people from a wide variety of backgrounds. Schools must consider the different cultural and religious needs of their students, and try to ensure everyone knows something about everyone else's background. Learning about festivals and carnivals can be a good way to achieve this.

Schools are one of the most important places to experience and learn about multiculturalism.

Extra help

Schools have to think particularly hard about how to help immigrant children integrate into their new school environment. These students may arrive with little knowledge of the language of the host country, and are given additional language classes to help them catch up with the school curriculum. Extra language classes are often also seen as the main tool in helping immigrant children fit into school life.

A TYPICAL STORY: BEING BULLIED

Children of immigrants often face the pressure of parental expectations that they do well at school. If other pupils pick on them, as happened to this young Bengali in Toronto, Canada, they may want to reject their family background completely.

"A bunch of bigger boys were waiting for their target. Since he didn't show up, and since I unknowingly walked by the 'battleground' I was beaten up. My new jacket [was] ripped in pieces, drenched in saliva... The following weeks I was bullied more, for what I thought was because I was brown. So then came my 'white days'. I would detest talking Bangla in public. I could never bring this up at the dinner table, and my other white friends dismissed the whole situation... I was a total mess."

Teachers try to ensure that all pupils feel included, whatever their backgrounds.

Difficult start

In Europe some immigrant communities find it particularly hard to be accepted. Many Islamic immigrants from Asia and Africa, for example, often end up unemployed and living in run-down housing areas. The children of these immigrants may also struggle to create opportunities for themselves, especially if there are language problems or they clash with the cultural expectations of their families. But difficult experiences can help young people, like Aïcha, become stronger.

AÏCHA'S STORY: DOUBLE PERSONALITY

Aïcha's parents emigrated from Algeria to France in the 1950s. Aïcha was born and educated in France. Coming from a family with very traditional values, her parents restricted her movements when she became a teenager. She began to feel trapped and alienated from her parents' culture, and no longer felt herself to be a Muslim. In her book, *Born In France*, she describes how that felt:

"I continuously saw myself as someone with a double personality. There was the person that was at home – the person my parents wanted me to be – a kind of transitory person. And there was the other person – elsewhere, but that was the one which was really me – the person whose veil I discarded one day."

27

The fight for equality

In any multicultural society it is vital that everyone has the same opportunities to access rights and opportunities. The basic principle of equality was set out in the United Nations Universal Declaration of Human Rights in 1949 – an important international moral code to which most countries have signed up. Yet until 1960s black people in the USA were still unequal compared to their white counterparts in the eyes of the law. They could not vote, had to send their children to separate schools, and even had to sit away from white people on buses and trains.

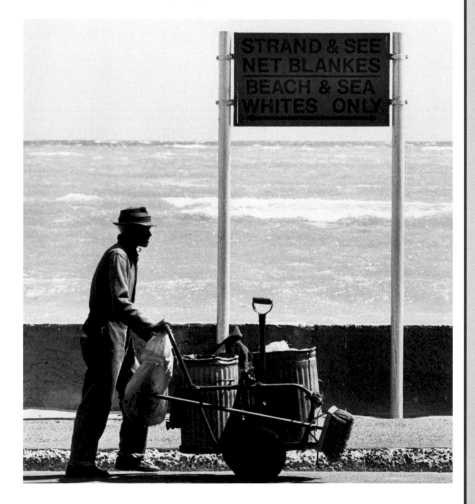

A black man passes a "whites only" sign in South Africa in 1988. Between the 1930s and the 1990s South Africa created Apartheid – one of the severest systems of racial segregation in the world.

JOHN A POWELL'S STORY: EARLY EXPERIENCES OF RACISM

John is a leading scholar in the USA on race and race equality issues. In an interview he described his experiences growing up in inner-city Detroit, as white families moved out to the suburbs when black families moved in.

"I was born in 1947, so I watched Detroit go from a vibrant city to starting to empty out. I watched my mother and father struggling to hold the family together and trying to get housing, and I remember the frustration. And then watching the city starting to die, and literally watching the complexion of the city change. I remember moving to an integrated neighbourhood that within a few years became an all-black neighbourhood... I also remember being bussed to school, and fighting on the playground because the white kids didn't want us there. I have all these memories. At first they were just experiences, and I didn't quite know how to make sense of them, and didn't necessarily think of them in racial terms, but as I got older and reflected on them, I began to understand."

An ambulance control centre. Jobs should be open to anyone, regardless of their ethnic background.

Equality in law

In developed countries, anti-race discrimination laws exist to ensure equality and to give people a way to challenge any disadvantages or injustices they may have suffered because of their different ethnic or cultural backgrounds. These laws mean that, in theory, no one is allowed to be discriminated against, harassed or in any way abused because of their skin colour, religion or place of birth.

Discrimination in practice

The existence of such laws does not, of course, stop discrimination from happening. American research, for example, shows that black and Hispanic people in the USA are still far more likely to be targeted by the police than white Americans. This means they are more likely to be arrested, too. Yet statistics show that there is no more likelihood of black and Hispanic people committing crimes than their white counterparts.

SILVIA'S STORY: GETTING JUSTICE

Silvia is Latin American and worked illegally as a secretary for an insurance company in San Francisco. When her employer failed to pay her wages, and working conditions became intolerable, Silvia filed a legal claim for the money she was owed. To retaliate, her employer informed the US immigration authorities that Silvia had worked illegally. But a court in California found that she was entitled to her wages. It also said that it was not acceptable for employers to retaliate in this way.

29

Equality and work

Finding work and improving career opportunities is an important area where equality laws can have a direct impact on the lives of members of ethnic minorities and immigrant communities. Research shows that immigrants, for example, are far less likely to find work than the local population. This makes it difficult for them to access further education, move out from the impoverished areas they often live in, and improve their standard of life.

DENG'S STORY: WANTING TO WORK

When Deng returned to his home country, Sudan, after studying at Cairo University, he had to flee to avoid being forcefully recruited into the Sudanese army. He came to the UK and applied for asylum. Even though he was allowed to work, finding a job was impossible.

"When I arrived in the UK in 1994, I was very keen to put my skills and qualifications to good use. As well as my studies in Egypt, I had an MA in second language curriculum development, and more than ten years' experience of teaching and translation work in both Egypt and Sudan. However, I found it almost impossible to find a job here, even though the Home Office had given me permission to work. Although I wrote over one hundred job applications, I only got one interview, and even then I was unsuccessful."

Today, Deng has permission to remain in the UK. He works for a charity to help other refugees in similar situations.

Positive action

In many developed countries it is illegal for an employer to give a job to a white person if there is a person from an ethnic minority who is more qualified to do the job. It is also illegal for employers to treat a person unfairly because of who they are. Some companies have r   t actively encourage people from   orities to apply for jobs.

e perceptions

Fear about immigration can make it harder for first, second and third generation immigrants to enter the job market. Negative reporting in the media often fuels people's perception that the arrival of immigrants is not good for society. It can lead to assumptions that immigrants lack qualifications or talent, and are only in the country to live off benefits. In direct contrast, many governments are now openly acknowledging that immigrant communities contribute hugely to the economy.

AS A MATTER OF FACT

Governments in some developed countries recognise that immigrants make important contributions to their economies. Most immigrants are of working age, are highly motivated to work and therefore pay taxes. Immigrants' financial contributions are difficult to work out but the UK government has estimated that immigrants pay £2.5 billion more in taxes than they get in benefits.

In Western countries many senior-level jobs are still dominated by white people. Equality works in theory, but often not in practice.

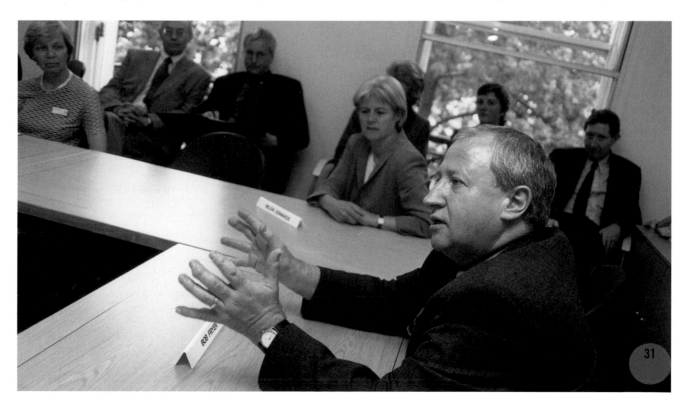

Understanding difference

Multicultural societies are marked by their religious diversity. Many developed countries are no longer home to one dominant religion, such as Christianity, but a variety of faiths, including Islam, Judaism, Hinduism, Buddhism and Sikhism. The benefits of a "multifaith" society include the possibility of people with different religions being enriched by each other's beliefs and traditions, and working together on international issues such as helping the victims of the Asian tsunami in 2004 or dealing with poverty in Africa.

Children performing a dance to mark the Hindu festival of Holi.

DYAB ABOU JAHJAH'S STORY: PUTTING THE RECORD STRAIGHT

Dyab Abou Jahjah is 31. He was born in Lebanon and now lives in Belgium. He was accused of inciting street riots in Antwerp after a mentally ill Belgian man had murdered a Muslim Moroccan schoolteacher. Abou Jahjah is very critical of European governments' attitude towards their Islamic communities:

"America's race laws are more advanced than here. I have relatives in Detroit and they are Arab Americans but they feel American. I don't feel European. Europe needs to make its concept of citizenship inclusive to all cultures and religions. I'm a practising Muslim but I'm not a freak. I'm not a fundamentalist."

Religious tensions

Different religions, however, can cause considerable tension within communities. Ever since the terrorist attacks in the USA on 11 September, 2001, some people in Western countries have viewed Islam with suspicion. One charge levelled at Muslims is that they are religious fanatics who support violent activities to promote their faith. In fact, like any religion, fanatics are only a tiny minority among Muslim people.

Different practices

Different religious practices have also caused debate and even court actions. Muslim girls and women in Britain and France, for example, have had to fight for their right to wear the hijab, the traditional Muslim headscarf. The charge of religious persecution is one that Western governments must take very seriously – their laws and constitutions commit them to ensuring all religions are allowed freedom of expression.

Turkish women in Berlin, Germany, wearing Muslim headscarves. Some people argue that the scarves should not be worn in non-religious schools.

JOANNE'S STORY: NEW VALUES

Joanne was brought up as a French-speaking Catholic in Canada in the 1950s. She tells how new values began to replace old ones.

"Neighborhoods became ethnically diverse and children began to speak English outside the home....[Then] the turbulent sixties changed a lot of traditions, customs and a way of life. Our church began celebrating mass in both languages. More mixed marriages were occurring within the family and the churches seem to acquire a more tolerant attitude."

Arranged marriages

As immigration from non-European countries has increased in developed countries, ethnic groups from certain African and Asian countries have brought with them cultural practices that clash with Western values. It is, for example, common for African and Asian families to arrange the marriages of their children. This practice can cause difficulties for young people, who are faced with balancing the wishes of their parents against the liberal ideas of Western society.

A Indian couple on their wedding day.

PAVI'S STORY: MY MOTHER'S ARGUMENT

Pavi, who is from a Hindu family, was opposed to having an arranged marriage. Here she discusses her mother's reasons why such a marriage was a good idea:

"My parents always felt it was so much better to first be married, and within that covenant context, learn to love each other. I didn't want to have an arranged marriage, and we had all kinds of debate on the matter. My mother's argument was that she had given birth to me, raised me, knew me inside and out, even though I thought I was all grown up and mature, and loved me like nobody else ever could – plus she understood women better than I did, and knew the realities of marriage from the inside. So who better to find me someone who would be a perfect fit?"

34

Honour killings

For immigrant women from different cultures, adapting to life in the West can be particularly difficult. They are often expected to conform to traditional roles and values in the family, may have very little contact with the outside world and may not learn the language of their home country. There have been cases in developed countries where husbands and brothers have even killed a female family member for not conforming to traditional values and bringing shame onto the family.

FADIME'S STORY: A FAMILY TRAGEDY

Fadime Sahindal immigrated to Sweden with her Turkish Kurdish family in the 1980s. She was 26 when her father shot her dead because she refused an arranged marriage and had a relationship with a Swedish man. Before her death in 2002, Fadime appealed for help and even spoke in the Swedish parliament about her situation:

"My parents' view was that family and relatives were the centre of things, and I therefore had to think about what was best for the family before thinking about my own well-being... But in contrast to my parents, I lived in and was part of Swedish society. I went to Swedish school every day, I ate Swedish food, I had Swedish friends and watched Swedish television. I therefore began to stretch the boundaries more and more... [and] continued to meet my Swedish friends."

Fitting in

Many different cultural practices are, however, easily absorbed into the fabric of multicultural societies. Some practices move beyond ethnic communities into the mainstream. Examples include the African and Caribbean traditions of carnival, the origins of which lie in West African celebrations and festivals held by slaves, and the Asian practices of vegetarianism, meditation, yoga and martial arts.

The Notting Hill Carnival, shown here, has had a big impact on British culture. Up to 1 million people attend the carnival, in West London, each year.

A question of identity

Most of us at some point in our lives will question what our identity is. For different people it can mean very different things. For immigrants, the question of identity can be a difficult one. Many will continue to feel a loyalty to their own country despite living in another country for many years. Their readiness to integrate into their new surroundings can also depend on why they left. Many refugees struggle to come to terms with the changes they have gone through.

A mother and son prepare food for the Muslim festival of Eid al-Adha ("feast of the sacrifice").

VAIRA VIKE-FREIBERGA'S STORY: FEELING LOST

Vaira Vike-Freiberga's family fled from Latvia to Canada when the Soviet Union invaded Latvia during the Second World War. In 1997 Vaira, a psychology professor, returned to Latvia and two years later was elected as its president. In a speech to mark the 50th anniversary of the Refugee Convention – the international law that protects refugees worldwide – she described the identity crisis many refugees experience:

"You are living outside of space and of time, you have no roots, you have no past, you don't know whether you have a future, you have no rights, you have no papers, sometimes you haven't even got your name and you have to pinch yourself to reassure yourself that yes, I am alive, I am me, I am a human being, I am a person. Do I count in this world? I don't know, I'll wait until tomorrow."

Between two cultures

Young people in immigrant communities usually find it easier than their parents to adapt to a Western lifestyle and identify with their new country. They mix with locals at school and tend to have a better knowledge of the country's language and a desire to do well in the future. For some, this can lead to them wanting to reject their family's culture. Others, like Jennifer (see panel), rediscover their own cultural heritage as they grow older.

Vietnamese American teenagers in California. Children of immigrants are often good at mixing their families' customs with mainstream culture.

JENNIFER'S STORY: A DEEP CONNECTION

Jennifer is in her early 30s and emigrated from South Korea to the USA when she was six. She went back to Korea to study and was keen to learn more about the country of her birth.

"There are many Koreans all around the world who miss their homeland. This is wonderful. However, I was very deeply disappointed by the fact that Koreans are not at all interested in these visiting students. While I was studying Korean history in graduate school in Korea, I was so surprised by the number of countries from which second generation Koreans came. Even though Koreans are scattered across the entire world, they still have a deep sense of home. What a joy that there are so many second and third generation Koreans who feel so deeply about Korea!"

Motivation

The ability to integrate today, as in the past, depends on motivation. Researchers have found that while local people have become very aware of their rights and may demand better pay and working conditions, immigrants are often different. They are less concerned about their rights in terms of benefits and work obligations, and more concerned about having a job – even if the pay is low – to get a foothold in the job market and to get ahead. Often they succeed and this makes them identify strongly with their new country.

37

The importance of citizenship

For immigrants wanting to be a part of the societies in which they now live, becoming a citizen is an important process. Citizenship gives immigrants the rights to vote, to stand for elections, and to be protected by their government when they travel abroad. Western countries have introduced citizenship tests for immigrants who want to become nationals. These test language skills, but also the level of knowledge of the history and culture of the country. Many immigrants feel very proud to be able to take the test and become a citizen in this way.

New US citizens taking the oath of loyalty on Ellis Island, New York.

JETTE'S STORY: TAKING THE AMERICAN OATH

Many countries also require their new citizens to take an oath of loyalty. Jette, who left Denmark in 1988 to join her husband in the USA, did just that.

"February 1, 1997 turned out to be the day that I finally took the oath. We set out on a crisp Saturday morning with 346 other people bearing exotic names from all over the world. We came in all shades of pink and brown, but the unifying characteristics were our bated breaths, shivering hands, and pounding hearts, realising this was it. We could still have changed our minds and run out as fast as we could, but everyone seemed determined, encouraged by the many smiling friends and family members who had come to share this important moment in our lives... Do I feel differently now? Not really. I still count and do math in Danish, I still have to spell my name and I still have to account for my accent now and again. What IS different is that when [the] President gets up and starts a speech with the words 'My fellow Americans' I feel I belong here."

New identities

For many people, identity is less about the decision to integrate into the mainstream or remain true to their parents' and grandparents' culture. It is more about shaping new identities that reflect both their family backgrounds and the place they live in today. These identities are reflected in descriptions such as "Greek Australian", "Mexican American" and "Black British". There are many songs, films and books that express what it is to have a mixed identity, informed by one's past, present and hopes for the future.

A diverse crowd watching a concert in the Barbes-Rochechouart district of Paris, France, which is home to many North African immigrants.

SHANE'S STORY: MIXED ORIGINS

Shane's father is a white American and his mother's parents are of black and Native American origin respectively. He is proud of his racial heritage, but can get frustrated by people's attitudes:

"People think I'm Greek, Italian, Puerto Rican, every damn thing under the sun, Panamanian, Argentinean, Serbian, Jewish. In New York, more cosmopolitan people realise there are shades of gray. And where I'm from you're black, you're white, or you're Indian. That's it. You're one or the other... Why is it that I have to explain things to white and blacks? Why can't I look at you as an individual and your characteristics as something more than your race? Race is a problem because people make it a problem. Just get on with it – get over it."

The multicultural future

A continuing dilemma

Societies in developed countries continue to face a dilemma. On the one hand, they accept cultural diversity and advantages that multiculturalism can bring. On the other hand, they are concerned about levels of immigration and the tensions this can create between different groups. Some people argue that it is down to each of us to accept how other people want to live. As Camilla suggests, "other people" want the same as everyone else – to fit in.

CAMILLA'S STORY: WHERE DO I FIT IN?

Camilla is a writer living in the USA. She was born in South Korea but was adopted and educated in Norway. Here she describes her thoughts on adapting to different cultures.

"When people ask me: 'Where you're from?' I've answered: 'I'm from Norway, but I was born in South Korea.' And sometimes to avoid further questions, I've also answered, 'I'm from South Korea.' This is a very typical reaction among Korean adoptees in Norway or other European countries.

"I grew up with four other siblings, one Norwegian brother and two sisters, and one other Korean adopted sister.

"Being adopted means to relate to being different in many ways. I think what I really want to say is that being different in terms of not being 'normal' or looking normal (meaning Norwegian, blonde, Scandinavian) is also a question of relating to what is different around you. You have to accept that others think you are from China, because you are from a different place. And if it's not China, what place is it? And how do I feel about it?

"By acknowledging this, I'm showing that it is possible to explore this unknown place that you have inside you, a place you might have forgotten until now. But whatever answers you might find about your cultural inheritance, your memories, and so on, they will always generate new questions, new territories to explore. It's all a matter of getting a grasp of life itself."

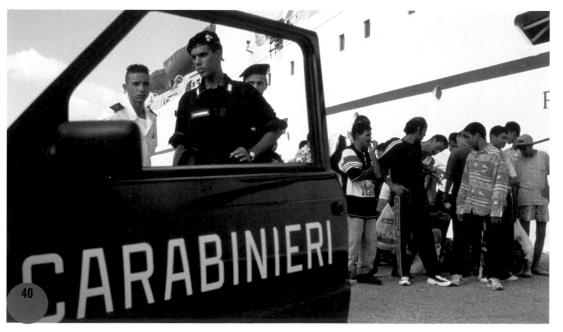

Italian policemen question new arrivals. Fears about immigration can stop people from seeing the good things different cultures bring to societies.

Integration or preservation

Some politicians maintain that ethnic minority communities should do more to integrate into Western societies. Such thinking has led many European countries, including Britain, the Netherlands and Denmark, to consider ways of encouraging integration. The Netherlands, for example, is looking into setting up special tests for non-Western immigrants to see whether they are making efforts to integrate. Immigrants would have to show that they are competent in the Dutch language and also understand the cultural norms of Dutch society.

A changing world

Multiculturalism, however, makes it harder to pin down the cultural norms of a particular country that everyone should accept. This trend is set only to increase. Governments acknowledge the economic importance of immigrants, so it is unlikely immigration will stop. And, whatever our backgrounds, we have all become citizens in a multicultural world, thanks to the Internet, digital television and global travel – as well as the experience of living with people whose backgrounds may be very different to our own.

Neighbours chatting on a street corner. It is up to each of us to accept and learn from other people.

Glossary

asylum Special legal immigration status given to people who are recognised as refugees according to the 1951 Convention on Refugees.

asylum seeker A person seeking asylum in another country because they fear persecution or danger in their own country.

British Empire The territories controlled by Britain from the 17th to mid-20th century as it expanded trade and conquered new lands. At its height, the British Empire covered almost 40 per cent of the world's land.

citizenship If a person has a country's citizenship, it means he or she is a national of that country and holds that country's passport.

colonisation The process of establishing a new settlement or colony, usually overseas from a home country.

colony Usually refers to an area of land controlled by a state that is overseas or abroad from it.

developed countries High-income countries where people have a high standard of living. These are usually found in Europe and North America, but include Australia, New Zealand and Japan.

developing countries Low- and middle-income countries where people have a lower standard of living and not as many goods and services available to them than in developed countries.

discrimination Treating people differently, and usually unfairly, because of their age, sex, nationality, colour or because of a disability.

economic growth When the production of goods and services increases, more profit is being made and more jobs are created.

emigrant A person leaving their home country to live permanently in another country.

European Union The union of 25 European countries which aims to work towards shared economic and social goals.

exploitation In a workplace situation, treating employees in a way that suits the interests of the business without respecting the interests of the individual.

fanatic People are fanatic if they are too enthusiastic or even obsessive about what they believe in or support, such as a religion, a pop star or a football club.

freeman A person who enjoys all the privileges of being a free citizen.

fundamentalist A person who supports a religion or a political party with such extreme enthusiasm that they do not like others to criticise their cause.

human rights Set of rights which everyone in the world should be entitled to, such as the right to free speech, the right to basic education and the right to move freely to other countries.

immigrant A person who has moved permanently to another country to live and work.

immigration laws Laws which set out the circumstances under which people can live and work in a country not their own.

integrate To adapt to the values and customs of the society in which one lives.

liberal A person is liberal when he or she is open-minded and tolerant of other people's opinions and supports the idea of individual freedom and democracy.

migrant A person going to work in another country usually for a limited time only.

missionary A person who is sent by a church to another area or country to promote its religion. Modern-day missionaries often carry out humanitarian work, such as helping the poor.

persecution Being punished, tortured or mistreated by a government or a military group, usually because of your political or religious beliefs or ethnic backround.

racism Judging people or behaving unfairly to them because of their skin colour or ethnic background.

refugees People living abroad who are recognised under international law as being unable to return to their home country for fear of their lives or freedom.

refugee camp A settlement, usually temporary, that develops when people flee their homes at times of war or famine to a safer area near the borders of their own country.

rights Claims to freedom, equal treatment and resources that are guaranteed by law.

Second World War The biggest world conflict in history, involving most of the world's countries, fought from 1939 until 1945.

visa Official permission from a foreign country to visit it. This is usually given by the country's embassy, who puts a stamp in a person's passport to show that a visa has been granted.

work ethic Believing in the personal benefits and advantages of carrying out work diligently and thoroughly.

Web connections

International Organisations

International Organisation for Migration (IOM)
www.iom.int

International Labour Organisation (ILO)
www.ilo.org

United Nations (UN)
www.un.org

United Nations High Commissioner for Refugees (UNHCR)
www.unhcr.ch

Non-governmental organisations

Anti-Slavery International
www.antislavery.org
Oldest human rights organisation set up in 1839 to campaign against slavery and forced labour.

Australian Refugee Council
www.refugeecouncil.org.au
Covers information about asylum and refugees in Australia.

British Refugee Council
www.refugeecouncil.org.uk
Leading refugee charity in the UK helping newly arrived asylum seekers and recognised refugees.

Civil Rights
www.civilrights.org
A US-based organisation which provides an on-line forum to work against discrimination in all its forms and building up public understanding towards social and economic justice.

Independent Race and Refugee Network
www.irr.org.uk
An independent educational charity carrying out research on race relations issues worldwide.

Minority Rights Group
www.minorityrights.org
A human rights organisation which works for the rights of minorities worldwide and to promote cooperation between communities.

Survival International
www.survival-international.org
An organisation that helps tribal people defend their lives, protect their lands and determine their own futures.

43

Index

Adams, Abigail 14
Adams, John 14
Africa 15, 23, 24, 27, 32, 35
Alexander the Great 10
Algeria 27
ancient Greeks 10
Apartheid 25, 28
Argentina 12
arranged marriages 34, 35
arts, the 8, 22, 23, 25
Asia 15, 27
asylum 30
Australia 16, 17, 18
Australasia 9

Belgium 32
Britain 10, 15, 19, 33, 35, 41
Buddhism 32

Canada 16, 18, 22, 26, 33, 36
Caribbean 14, 19, 35
China 11
Christianity 12, 32
citizenship 38
civil war 19
colonies 19
colonisation 10, 12, 13, 14, 15
cultural
   backgrounds 8, 18
   diversity 8, 18, 23, 40
   identity 13, 23, 39
   minority 8
   tensions 9
culture 8, 11, 16, 20, 24
   Roman 10
customs 8, 10, 37

Denmark 21, 22, 38, 41
developed countries 21, 27, 29, 31, 32, 34, 40
discrimination 15, 29
   laws 29

economy 14, 31, 41
   benefits to 20, 41
   difficulties with 19
education 18, 26, 28, 30, 34
Egypt 30
employment 30, 31
England 19, 24
equality 28, 30, 31
ethnic
   background 29
   communities 16, 21, 22, 24, 35
   group 9, 11, 21, 34
   minority 9, 20, 21, 22, 30, 31, 41
Europe 9, 13, 14, 16, 19

family 8, 17, 18, 22, 24, 28, 34, 35, 38, 39
food 12, 25, 34
France 19, 27, 33, 39

Germany 33
Giles, Herbert A 11
Great Wall of China, the 11

Han dynasty, the 11
Hinduism 24, 32, 34

identity 23, 36, 39
immigrant communities 18, 27, 30, 37, 41
immigrants 16, 17, 19, 22, 26, 27, 31, 34
immigration patterns 9
India 10, 15, 24
integration 26, 36, 37, 39, 41
Islam 21, 27, 32, 33, 36
Italy 10

Judaism 32

language 8, 10, 11, 15, 21, 23, 26, 27, 30, 37, 38, 41

Lebanon 32
Lønvenskjold, Adam 13

Macaulay, Thomas 15
Middle East 9, 24
multicultural society 8, 9, 22, 25, 32, 35
multiculturalism 9, 10, 20, 26, 40, 41
Muslim See Islam

Netherlands, the 41
North Africa 9
North America 13, 14
Norway 40

persecution 13, 16, 23, 33
police 21, 29, 40
Powell, John A 28
prejudice 17, 20

Qichao, Liang 17

race 9, 15, 28, 39
racial segregation 28
racism 18, 21, 28
Refugee Convention 36
refugees 21, 22, 30, 36
religious
   diversity 32
   tension 33
rights 14, 28, 37, 38

school 14, 19, 26, 28, 35, 37
Second World War 19
Sikhism 32
slave trade 14, 15
society 8, 10
   multicultural 8, 9, 22, 25, 32, 35
   Western 20, 23, 31, 34, 38
South Africa 9, 25, 28
South America 15, 16
South Korea 37, 40
Soviet Union 36
sport 25

Sudan 30
Sweden 35

trade 9, 10
Turkey 10, 22, 23

UK (United Kingdom) 19, 30, 31
United Nations Declaration of Human Rights 28
USA (United States of America) 9, 13, 15, 16, 17, 18, 25, 28, 29, 33, 37, 38, 40

Wichî Indian 12